The Confessions
of a
Victorious Believer

The Confessions

of a

Victorious Believer

by
Aaron Jones

A BOLD TRUTH Publication
Christian Literature & Artwork

Unless otherwise indicated all Scripture quotations are taken from the King James Version of The Bible.

Contents

Recommendations

"Aaron is my personal friend in the ministry, I have nick-named him "dunamis." Because the healing power of God and the gifts of the Holy Ghost flow mightily through him, when a demand of faith is placed upon the Lord Jesus Christ when he shares God's Word."

Daryl P. Holloman
Rhema Missionary, Doho, Qatar

"Aaron has a heart for the unlearned people in the remotest re-gions of the globe. God has given him a unique visual means of reaching them with the blood covenant truth of the gospel."

David Manuel
Bestselling Author, Boston, Mass.

It is my privilege to recommend to you the ministry of Rev. Aaron Jones. I know Aaron to be a gifted artist, a passionate minister, and a missionary strategist. His desire to see indi-vidual lives changed, and to affect leadership by the power of God that permeates everything he does.

Dr. Dave Leggett
President, Tulsa Chapter
Full Gospel Businessmen Fellowship International

SOME POWERFUL THINGS
for Christians to think about

~

The Names of God

Adonai — Our Sovereign Lord
Elohim — The Eternal Creator
El-Elyon — The Lord Most High
*El-Shaddai — The God of More Than Enough
Jehovah-Jireh — The Lord our Provider
Jehovah –Nissi — The Lord our Banner
Jehovah-Ropheka — The Lord our Healer
Jehovah-Shalom — The Lord our Peace
Jehovah-Tsidkenu — The Lord our Righteousness
Jehovah-Shammah — The Lord is Present
Jehovah-Sabaoth — The Lord of Hosts
Jehovah-Rohi — The Lord our Shepherd

*King James Version translates El-Shaddai as
God Almighty

~

10 things God will do for you.

1. Supernatural increase and promotion

2. Prominence and preferential treatment

3. Victories in the face of impossible odds

4. Honor in the midst of your adversaries

5. Restoration of everything the enemy has stolen from us

6. Recognition when you seem to be the least likely

7. Petitions granted by both ungodly and Godly civil authorities

8. Policies, rules, regulations and laws reversed or changed to my advantage

9. Increase in material wealth especially Real Estate

10. You don't have to fight the battle, Jesus fought it for you and the battle is already WON!!!

Pray these out loud every day, request them every day, and expect them to be fulfilled in your life.

Surely goodness and mercy shall follow me all the days of my life... Psalm 23:6

~

"We have a God who delights in impossibilities." ~ Billy Sunday

~

"Faith is to rest, not in the best of God's servants, but in His unchanging Word." ~ H. A. Ironside

~

Always remember to feed on God's Word daily.

There is no substitute for spending time with God
in His written Word - The Bible.

∿

Be strong and courageous,
BE NOT AFRAID nor dismayed

Dr. Lester Sumrall said he armed himself with
the following passage of scriptures and traveled all
around the world, preaching the gospel,
healing the sick and casting out devils.

Fear thou not; for I am with thee:
be not dismayed; for I am thy God:
I will strengthen thee; yea, I will help thee;
yea, I will uphold thee with
the right hand of my righteousness.
Behold, all they that were incensed against thee
shall be ashamed and confounded:
they shall be as nothing;
and they that strive with thee shall perish.
Thou shalt seek them, and shalt not find them,
even them that contended with thee:
they that war against thee shall be as nothing,
and as a thing of nought.
(Isaiah 41:10-13)

Have you READ THE BIBLE lately? IT HAS NOT CHANGED, it is still the same eternal truth that men and women have built SUCCESSFUL LIVES, FAMILIES and BUSINESSES on for Centuries.

∼

"Never count people out until the Holy Spirit tells you to walk away. God is in the business of restoring broken lives."

∼

"I prayed for Faith, and thought that some day Faith would come down and strike me like lightning. But Faith did not seem to come. One day I read in the tenth chapter of Romans, 'Now Faith cometh by hearing, and hearing by the Word of God'. I had closed my Bible, and prayed for Faith. I now opened my Bible, and began to study, and Faith has been growing ever since. "
~D.L. Moody

∼

"Nothing can touch the Word of God. Not all the powers of earth and hell, men and devils combined, can ever move the Word of God. There it stands, in its own moral glory, spite of all the assaults of the enemy, from age to age. 'For ever, O Lord, Thy Word is settled in heaven.'" ~C.H. Mackintosh

NOTE: All Scriptures marked with ✟ are direct quotes from The Holy Bible.

Some confessions may be repeated as are many of the promises in The Word of God.

The Confessions of a Victorious Believer

from the Old Testament

"I am created in the image of God."
Genesis 1:27

"Whatever I call things, that is what they are."
Genesis 2:19, Mk. 11:23, Ro. 4:17

"There is nothing to hard for my God."
Genesis 18:14

"I am a prosperous man."
Genesis 39:2, 3, 23

"People around me are blessed for my sake."
Genesis 39:5

"I have supernatural favour with the world's
economic system."
Exodus 3:21, 11:3, 12:36

"The blood is a token of my salvation to me."
Exodus 12:13

"The Lord continues to heal me."
Exodus 15:26

"The Lord has given me a good land."
Deuteronomy 1:25, 6:18

"My house is full of good things."
Deuteronomy 6:11

"God cast all my enemies out before me."
Deuteronomy 6:19

"My silver and gold, and all that I have
is continually being multiplied."
Deuteronomy 8:13

"God has given me power to get wealth."
Deuteronomy 8:18

"I will teach God's Words to my children."
Deuteronomy 11:19

"Everywhere I set my feet I possess."
Deuteronomy 11:24

"No man can stand before me."
Deuteronomy 11:25

"All is well with my children."
Deuteronomy 12:25

"I have a new house."
Deuteronomy 22:8

"My wallet and bank accounts are blessed."
Deuteronomy 28:5

"My enemies flee from me completely."
Deuteronomy 28:7

"The Lord has commanded the blessing on me."
Deuteronomy 28:8

"I am the head and not the tail."
Deuteronomy 28:13

"I serve the Lord with joyfulness
and gladness of heart."
Deuteronomy 28:47

"I ride on the high places of the earth."
Deuteronomy 32:13

"I have good courage."
Joshua 1:6

"I am prosperous and have good success."
Joshua 1:8

"The Lord has given me all the land."
Joshua 2:24

"I Shout! For the Lord has given me this city."
Joshua 6:16

"I have rest all around."
Joshua 21:44, 23:1

"I own land and cities that I did not labor for."
Joshua 24:13

"And Jabez called on the God of Israel, saying,
Oh that thou wouldest bless me indeed, and enlarge
my coast, and that thine hand might be with me,
and that thou wouldest keep me from evil,
that it may not grieve me!
And God granted him that which he requested."
I Chronicles 4:10

"I am waxing greater and greater."
I Chronicles 11:9

"He suffered no man to do them wrong: yea,
he reproved kings for their sakes,
Saying, touch not mine anointed,
and do my prophets no harm."
I Chronicles 16:21, 22

"The Lord will build me a house."
I Chronicles 17:10, 25

"God is with me and He will not forsake."
I Chronicles 28:20

"Our land is healed."
II Chronicles 7:14

"God shows Himself strong on my behalf."
II Chronicles 16:9

"I have much business."
II Chronicles 17:13

"There is much spoil when I win a battle."
II Chronicles 20:25

"I am delivered from those who would to do evil
to me on the road."
Ezra 8:31

"I fast and pray."
Nehemiah 1:4

"I cannot come down."
Nehemiah 6:3

"The work will not cease."
Nehemiah 6:3

"My hands are strong."
Nehemiah 6:9

"I am protected from weapons of war."
Job 5:20

"I am hid from verbal abuse."
Job 5:21

"I am not afraid of animals."
Job 5:22

"The longer I live, the more I increase."
Job 8:7

"I am aquainted with the Lord."
Job 22:21

"Only good comes on me."
Job 22:21

"I am built up."
Job 22:23

"I store up gold as dust."
Job 22:24

"I have plenty of money."
Job 22:25

"God's light shines on my pathway."
Job 22:28

"I pray for my friends."
Job 42:10

"Every man hands me money."
Job 42:11

"I have more than I started with of everything."
Job 42:12

"I am a blessed man."
Psalm 1:1, 5:12, Jer. 17:7

"I delight in the law of the Lord."
Psalm 1:2

"I am planted by the river of God's Word,
I am fruitful,
and everything I do prospers."
Psalm 1:3

"The heathen are my inheritance."
Psalm 2:8

"I own property and things all over the world."
Psalm 2:8

"God is my shield."
Psalm 3:3

"God hears me."
Psalm 3:4

"I am not afraid of ten thousand
that are set against me."
Psalm 3:6

"God smites all my enemies."
Psalm 3:7

"The blessing of the Lord is upon me."
Psalm 3:8

"God hears my prayer."
Psalm 4:3

"I trust in the Lord."
Psalm 4:5, 9:10, 11:1

"I lay down to sleep in peace,
God makes sure I am safe."
Psalm 4:8

"God's favor is wrapped around me like a shield."
Psalm 5:12

"All my enemies have been shamed."
Psalm 6:10

"God saves me from any and all that persecute me."
Psalm 7:1, 17:7

"My defence is of God."
Psalm 7:10

"God is mindful of me."
Psalm 8:4, 144:3

"I have dominion over all things."
Psalm 8:6

"I praise the Lord with all my heart."
Psalm 9:1

"God maintains my cause."
Psalm 9:2, 16:5

"The Lord is my refuge."
Psalm 9:9, 14:6

"God has lifted me from the gates of death."
Psalm 9:13

"Jesus is King forever."
Psalm 10:16

"The Lord helps me."
Psalm 12:1, 146:5

"God sets me in a safe place."
Psalm 12:5

"God keeps me from evil."
Psalm 12:7, Jo. 17:15

"The Lord preserves me."
Psalm 12:7, 16:1

"Jesus is my counselor and instructor."
Psalm 16:7

"God shows me the path of life."
Psalm 16:11

"I am joyful."
Psalm 16:11, Jo. 15:11, 16:24

"My mouth shall only speak right things."
Psalm 17:3

"God holds me up wherever I go."
Psalm 17:5

"I am the apple of God's eye."
Psalm 17:8, Zec. 2:8

""I am hid under the shadow of His wings."
Psalm 17:8

"God always delivers me from the wicked."
Psalm 17:13, 18:48

"The Lord is my strength."
Psalm 18:1

✝"The Lord is my rock, and my fortress,
and my deliverer; my God, my strength,
in whom I will trust; my buckler,
and the horn of my salvation, and my high tower.
I will call upon the Lord, who is worthy to be praised:
so shall I be saved from mine enemies."
Psalm 18:2, 3

"God has set me in a large place."
Psalm 18:19

"God has lit up that which was dark for me."
Psalm 18:28

"God sets me continually on high places."
Psalm 18:33

"God teaches me how to make war."
Psalm 18:34

"I have the shield of salvation."
Psalm 18:35

"I always overtake my enemies."
Psalm 18:37

"God subdues those that are against me."
Psalm 18:39, 47

"I am delivered from people's
struggles and arguments."
Psalm 18:43

"I am above those that would come against me."
Psalm 18:48

"God defends me."
Psalm 20:1

"God grants my every request,
and gives me my heart's desire."
Psalm 21:2

"Praise the Lord!"
Psalm 21:23, 26

✝ "The Lord is my shepherd; I shall not want.
He maketh me to lie down in green pastures:
he leadeth me beside the still waters.
He restoreth my soul: he leadeth me in the paths

of righteousness for his name's sake.
Thou preparest a table before me in the presence of
mine enemies: thou anointest my head with oil;
my cup runneth over.
Surely goodness and mercy shall follow me
all the days of my life:
and I will dwell in the house of the LORD for ever."
Psalm 23:1-6

"God will not let me be ashamed."
Psalm 25:2, 3

"My soul dwells at ease."
Psalm 25:13

"The Lord tells me heavenly secrets."
Psalm 25:14

"I am not in distress."
Psalm 25:17

"My sins are forgiven."
Psalm 25:18

"I have no trouble."
Psalm 25:22

"I will dwell in the house of the Lord
all the days of my life."
Psalm 27:4

"He has set me upon a Rock."
Psalm 27:5

"I see the goodness of the Lord."
Psalm 27:13, 145:9

"The Lord has healed me."
Psalm 30:2

"God has turned my mourning into dancing."
Psalm 30:11

"My time is in His hands."
Psalm 31:15

"Oh! How great is thy goodness."
Psalm 31:19

"The Lord has hidden me from arguments and strife."
Psalm 31:20

"My transgressions are covered."
Psalm 32:1

"I will bless the Lord at all times."
Psalm 34:1

"God has delivered me from all my fears."
Psalm 34:4

"I am delivered out of all trouble."
Psalm 34:6, 17, 19, 54:7

"The angel of the Lord encamps all around me."
Psalm 34:7

"I have no want or lack."
Psalm 34:9, 10

"Not one of my bones will be broken."
Psalm 34:20

"I will never be desolate."
Psalm 34:22

"God fights those who try to fight me."
Psalm 35:1

"Any enemies are confounded and put to shame."
Psalm 35:4, 26, 44:7, 71:24

"I do not fret over anyone or anything."
Psalm 37:1, 7

"God has given me the desires of my heart."
Psalm 37:4, 145:19

✞ "Commit thy ways unto the Lord;
trust also in him; and he shall bring it to pass."
Psalm 37:5

"My steps are ordered of the Lord."
Psalm 37:23

"I lend to others."
Psalm 37:26, 112:5

"The end result of all I do is peace."
Psalm 37:37

"I take heed to my own ways."
Psalm 39:1

"God has established my path."
Psalm 40:2

"Let the Lord be magnified!"
Psalm 40:16

"I am concerned about the poor."
Psalm 41:1

"My enemies do not triumph over me."
Psalm 41:11

"God is my health."
Psalm 43:5

"I have a clean heart and a right spirit inside me."
Psalm 51:10

"God will sustain me."
Psalm 55:22

"I am delivered from death."
Psalm 56:13

"God does all things for me."
Psalm 57:2

"I sing unto the Lord among the nations."
Psalm 57:9

"The banner of the Lord is over me."
Psalm 60:4

"I do valiantly."
Psalm 60:12

"My life is preserved and lengthened."
Psalm 61:6, 145:20, Pro. 9:11

✟ "He only is my rock and my salvation;
he is my defence;
I shall not be greatly moved."
Psalm 62:2

"My expectation is from God."
Psalm 62:5

"I am in a wealthy place."
Psalm 66:12

"I pay my vows."
Psalm 66:13, 116:14, 18

"God daily loads me with benefits."
Psalm 68:19

"I have strength and power."
Psalm 68:35

"I set on high."
Psalm 69:29

"My children are saved."
Psalm 72:4

"I fall down before Jesus, and serve Him."
Psalm 72:11

"God is good to me."
Psalm 73:1, 145:9

"God is strength to my physical heart."
Psalm 73:26

"God promotes me."
Psalm 75:6

"God leads me safely."
Psalm 78:53

"God doesn't withhold any good thing from me."
Psalm 84:11, 85:12

"My land yields increase."
Psalm 85:12, 144:13, 14

"I am holy."
Psalm 86:2

✟ "He that dwelleth in the secret place of the most
High shall abide under the shadow of the Almighty.
I will say of the LORD, He is my refuge
and my fortress: my God; in him will I trust.
Surely he shall deliver thee from
the snare of the fowler,
and from the noisome pestilence.
He shall cover thee with his feathers,
and under his wings shalt thou trust:
his truth shall be thy shield and buckler.
Thou shalt not be afraid for the terror by night;
nor for the arrow that flieth by day;
Nor for the pestilence that walketh in darkness;
nor for the destruction that wasteth at noonday.
A thousand shall fall at thy side, and ten thousand at
thy right hand; but it shall not come nigh thee.
Only with thine eyes shalt thou behold
and see the reward of the wicked.

Because thou hast made the Lord,
which is my refuge,
even the most High, thy habitation;
There shall no evil befall thee,
neither shall any plague come nigh thy dwelling.
For he shall give his angels charge over thee,
to keep thee in all thy ways.
They shall bear thee up in their hands,
lest thou dash thy foot against a stone.
Thou shalt tread upon the lion and adder:
the young lion and the dragon
shalt thou trample under feet.
Because he hath set his love upon me,
therefore will I deliver him: I will set him on high,
because he hath known my name.
He shall call upon me, and I will answer him:
I will be with him in trouble; I will deliver him,
and honour him. With long life will I satisfy him,
and show him my salvation."
Psalm 91:1-16

"I am flourishing."
Psalm 92:12-14

✝ "I will behave myself wisely in a perfect way."
Psalm 101:2

✝ "I will set no wicked thing before my eyes."
Psalm 101:3

"I am forgiven and healed."
Psalm 103:3

"My life is redeemed from destruction."
Psalm 103:4

"My youthful strength is renewed."
Psalm 103:5

"The earth is full of God's riches."
Psalm 104:24

"No man does me wrong."
Psalm 105:14

"God gives me my requests."
Psalm 106:15, 145:19

"I never murmur or complain."
Psalm 106:25, 144:14

"I say, I am redeemed."
Psalm 107:2

"He has sent His Word and healed me."
Psalm 107:20

"My children are mighty on the earth."
Psalm 112:2

"Wealth and riches are in my house."
Psalm 112:3

"I am not afraid of bad news."
Psalm 112:7

"I set with royalty."
Psalm 113:8

"I will increase more and more."
Psalm 115:14

"God has given me the earth."
Psalm 115:16

✞ "I will walk before the Lord in
the land of the living."
Psalm 116:9

"Jesus is on my side."
Psalm 118:6

"I shall not die, but live and declare
the works of the Lord."
Psalm 118:17

"I am living in prosperity."
Psalm 118:25

"I walk in liberty."
Psalm 119:45

✝ "Thy word is a lamp unto my feet,
and a light unto my path."
Psalm 119:105

"I am delivered from the oppression of men."
Psalm 119:134

"I have great peace."
Psalm 119:165

"I am preserved from all evil."
Psalm 121:7

"All is well with me and my family."
Psalm 128:2, 3

"I enjoy my grandchildren."
Psalm 128:6

"I have excess of provision."
Psalm 132:15

"I am in unity with my brothers in the Lord."
Psalm 133:1

"God gives me my food."
Psalm 136:25

"Jesus perfects everything that pertains to me."
Psalm 138:8

"God knows my thoughts."
Psalm 139:23

"God preserves me from violent men."
Psalm 140:1, 4

"The high praises of God are in my mouth."
Psalm 149:6

"I have wisdom, knowledge and understanding."
Proverb 1:2-4, 4:7

"I dwell safely."
Proverb 1:33

"I have length of days and long life."
Proverb 3:2

"I have favour and good understanding
in front of men."
Proverb 3:4

"I acknowledge the Lord in all I do."
Proverb 3:6

"My accounts are filled to capacity."
Proverb 3:10

"When I lay down, I am not afraid."
Proverb 3:24

"My path is a shining light."
Proverb 4:18

"I inherit many things, my treasure is full."
Proverb 8:21

"My mouth is a well of life."
Proverb 10:11, 13:2

"The Lord's blessing has made me rich."
Proverb 10:22

"I will leave an inheritance to my grandchildren."
Proverb 13:22

"I have many friends."
Proverb 14:20, 19:4

"My heart is sound."
Proverb 14:30

"There is much treasure in my house."
Proverb 15:6

"My enemies are at peace with me."
Proverb 16:7

"I have a merry heart."
Proverb 17:22

"Mercy and truth preserve me."
Proverb 20:28

"I have a good name."
Proverb 22:1

"My children will not depart from
the ways of the Lord."
Proverb 22:6

"I stand before kings."
Proverb 22:29

"All of my rooms are full of
riches and precious things."
Proverb 24:4

"I am bold as a lion."
Proverb 28:1

"I possess good things."
Proverb 28:10

"God has given me riches and wealth."
Ecclesiastes 5:19

"I am willing and obedient."
Isaiah 1:19

"I only eat the good of the land."
Isaiah 1:19

"I am not fainthearted."
Isaiah 7:4

"The anointing has destroyed the yoke off of me."
Isaiah 10:27

✞ "Thou wilt keep him in perfect peace,
whose mind is stayed on thee:
because he trusteth in thee."
Isaiah 26:3

"I stand for what is noble and generous."
Isaiah 32:8

"I sow finances and time into many people."
Isaiah 32:20

✞ "But they that wait upon the Lord shall renew their
strength; they shall mount up with wings as eagles;
they shall run, and not be weary;
and they shall walk, and not faint."
Isaiah 40:31

"God gives me treasures of darkness,
and hidden riches in secret places."
Isaiah 45:3

"I speak words in season."
Isaiah 50:4

"I have beautiful feet."
Isaiah 52:7

✟ "But he was wounded for my transgressions,
he was bruised for our iniquities:
the chastisement of our peace was upon him;
and with his stripes we are healed."
Isaiah 53:5

"I am breaking forth on the right hand
and on the left."
Isaiah 54:3

"All of my children are taught by the Lord and about
the Lord, and my children are in great peace."
Isaiah 54:13

"I am established in Righteousness.
I am in Right-standing with God
through Christ Jesus."
Isaiah 54:14

"I am far removed from oppression of any kind,

I do not fear anyone or anything.
I am far away from terror of any kind,
because it does not come near me."
Isaiah 54:14

"God is on my side, if anyone does come against me
they will fall defeated because I am in Christ."
Isaiah 54:15

"Absolutely no weapon that is formed or devised
against me will be successful, and every word spoken
against me to condemn or judge me, I will eventually
judge and the truth will come forth.
This is my heir's right as one of God servants."
Isaiah 54:17

"I have the righteousness of God."
Isaiah 54:17

"I go with joy and I am led by peace because God's
Word prospers and accomplishes everything He
sends it to do through me."
Isaiah 55:11, 12

"I trust in the Lord, and I possess the land."
Isaiah 57:13

"God knew me before I was born."
Jeremiah 1:5

"I am not afraid of the faces of men."
Jeremiah 1:8

"God always delivers me."
Jeremiah 1:8, 19

"No enemy can prevail against me."
Jeremiah 1:19

"It is well with me."
Jeremiah 7:23, 42:6

"I dwell where milk and honey flows freely."
Jeremiah 11:5

"I am redeemed out of the hand of the terrible."
Jeremiah 15:21

"I do not trust in the flesh."
Jeremiah 17:5

"I am healed."
Jeremiah 17:14

"His Word is like fire shut up in my bones."
Jeremiah 20:9

"Persecutors stumble and don't prevail against me."
Jeremiah 20:11

"My house is built in righteousness."
Jeremiah 22:13

"I fear no more."
Jeremiah 23:4

"I am not disheartened."
Jeremiah 23:4

"I do not lack."
Jeremiah 23:4

"God has His eyes on me for good."
Jeremiah 24:6

"I have an expected end."
Jeremiah 29:11

"My bonds have been broken off."
Jeremiah 30:8, Na. 1:13

"I rest and no one makes me afraid."
Jeremiah 30:10, Ezek. 34:28

"My health is restored
and my wounds have been healed."
Jeremiah 30:17

"Jehovah is my God."
Jeremiah 31:33

"I have the cure.
I have an abundance of peace and truth."
Jeremiah 33:6

"I tremble at the incredible goodness and prosperity
that the Lord has shown me."
Jeremiah 33:9

"God performs all the good things
that He promised me."
Jeremiah 33:14

"Because I trust the Lord, I will not fall by the sword."
Jeremiah 39:18

"God is with me to save me."
Jeremiah 42:11

"The Lord pleads my cause."
Jeremiah 50:34, Lam. 3:58

"The Lord is my portion."
Lamentations 3:24

"God has redeemed my life."
Lamentations 3:58

"I am not afraid of men's words."
Ezekiel 2:6

"I am not afraid of men."
Ezekiel 3:9, Lu. 12:4

"My wealth and renown is known
among the heathen."
Ezekiel 16:11-14

"I have confidence."
Ezekiel 28:26, II Co. 5:6, 8

"I receive showers of blessings."
Ezekiel 34:26

"God gives me wisdom and knowledge,
and I have understanding."
Daniel 2:21

"God reveals deep and secret things to me."
Daniel 2:22, 28

"I have an excellent spirit in me."
Daniel 6:3

"I am strong and do exploits
(signs, wonders and great works)."
Daniel 11:32

"I eat in plenty and am satisfied."
Joel 2:26

"I am strong."
Joel 3:10, Hag. 2:4

✞ "The Lord God is my strength,
and he will make my feet like hinds feet,
and he will make me walk upon mine high places…"
Habakkuk 3:19

✞ "The silver is mine and the gold is mine,
saith the Lord of hosts."
Haggai 2:8

"The Lord is a wall of fire around me."
Zechariah 2:5

"No oppressor comes near my house."
Zechariah 9:8

"The Lord of hosts defends me."
Zechariah 9:15

"There is a fountain of forgiveness opened to me."
Zechariah 13:1

"When I call on God, He hears me."
Zechariah 13:9

"The Sun of righteousness has risen over me
with healing in His wings."
Malachi 4:2

"I tread down the wicked."
Malachi 4:3

NOTES:_____

_____

_____

_____

_____

_____

_____

_____

_____

_____

_____

_____

_____

_____

_____

_____

_____

_____

PRAYER REQUESTS _____

_____

_____

_____

_____

_____

_____

_____

_____

_____

_____

_____

_____

_____

_____

_____

_____

_____

_____

CONFESSION _____

_____

_____

_____

_____

_____

_____

_____

_____

_____

_____

_____

_____

_____

_____

_____

_____

_____

_____

_____

_____

_____

_____

ANSWERED PRAYERS _____

_____

_____

_____

_____

_____

_____

_____

_____

_____

_____

_____

_____

_____

_____

_____

_____

_____

_____

_____

_____

Photos from some of our trips to the Nations.

PERU, SOUTH AMERICA

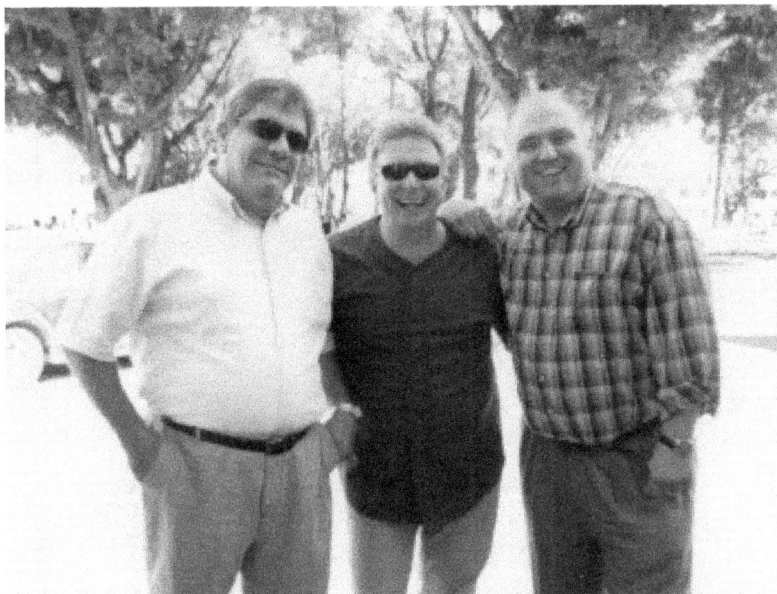

...with Rigoberto Perez and Terrell Glaze in Lima, Peru

The Mission's Team crawled in this VERY small plane in Peru

Ministering to God's Leaders in Huanaco, Peru

KENYA, EAST AFRICA

Some Kenyan Security I met and prayed with in Nairobi.

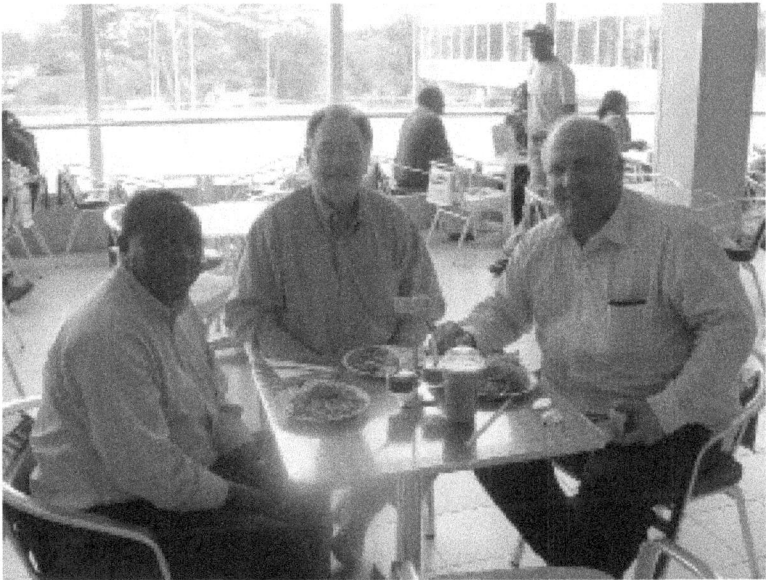

Some good fellowship and Chinese Food
with Bishop Paul Mbithi and Charles R. England

With Bishop David Sirma praying for a blind man
on the streets of Nairobi, Kenya.

The Gospel is worth shouting over, in Masailand, Kenya.

With my new Masai Brothers, in Masailand, Kenya.

Preaching with my interpreter Moses (Aaron & Moses)
Sometimes you just know it was God ordained!

With some of the Ladies from the Churches in Isinya, Kenya.

Evangelism to the Maasai in a remote area of Kenya.

Traveling and Ministering with Bishop David Sirma
in southern Kenya (Masailand)

Meeting with The Church of tomorrow in Isinya, Kenya.

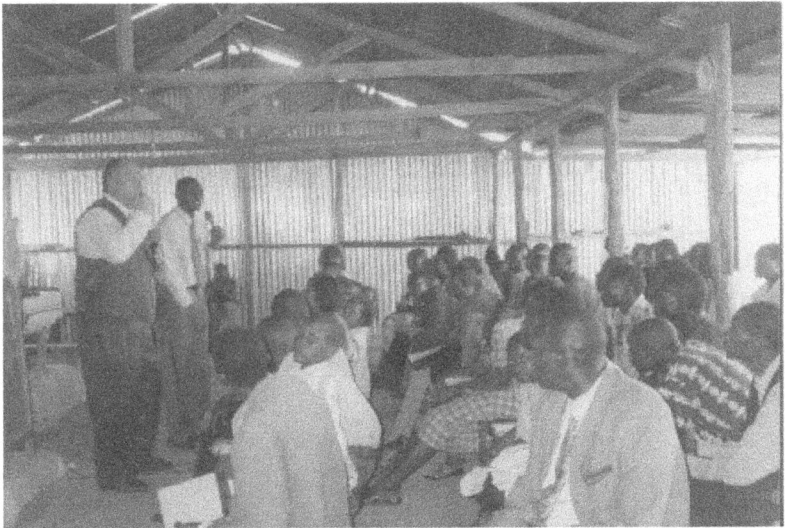

Preaching with Douglas Kulei in Isinya, Kenya.

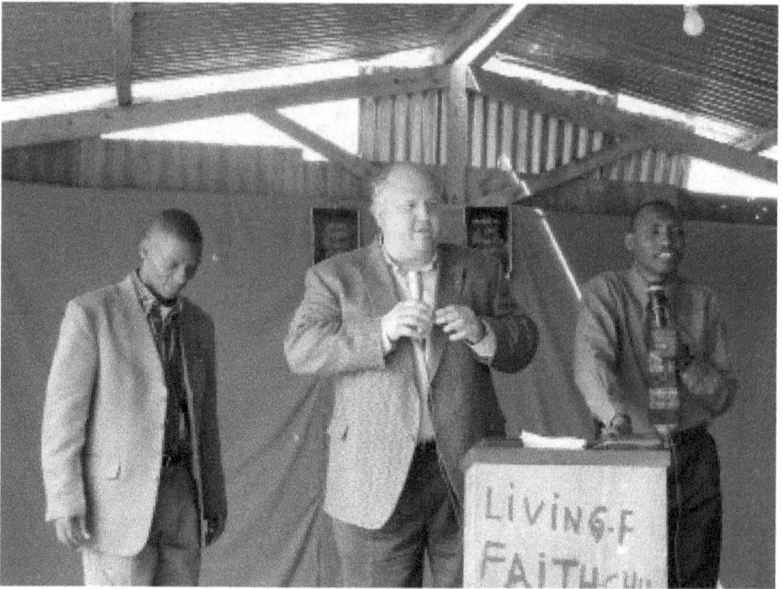

Ministering with Douglas Kulei and Apostle Ian Sebbanja.
What an honor to serve with these great Men of God!

A Parliment Member took us to lunch at the Serena Hotel.
God said, "The high places and the low places of the Nations."

OSLO, NORWAY

Preaching the Gospel in Norway's capital city, Oslo.

God opened a great door of opportunity to minister to all of Scandinavia via Christian Television while in Norway.

In Oslo, Norway meeetings with
Tallat Mohamed and Joar & Inger Haugland

Preaching with my good Friend and Brother Nils Pettersen.

Prayer and laying on hands.
God working to change lives in Oslo, Norway.

Being interviewed by Nils Pettersen on
Norwegian Christian Television.

Inside the soundbooth at the TV Studio.
Norwegian Christian Television.

Getting settled in for the long flight home.

The Confessions

of a

Victorious Believer

from the New Testament

"I have been filled with righteousness."
Matthew 5:6

"I rejoice and I am extremely happy."
Matthew 5:12

"Great is my reward in Heaven."
Matthew 5:12

"I am the light of the world."
Matthew 5:14

"My light shines."
Matthew 5:16

"I am called great in the Kingdom of heaven."
Matthew 5:19

"I am perfect."
Matthew 5:48

"My Father rewards me openly"
Matthew 6:4, 18

"God knows what I have need of."
Matthew 6:8

"God gives me my daily bread."
Matthew 6:11

"I am delivered from evil."
Matthew 6:13

"I forgive."
Matthew 6:14

"My treasure is in Heaven."
Matthew 6:20

"God dresses me very well, and supplies
all my material needs."
Matthew 6:28-33

"I seek the Kingdom of God first."
Matthew 6:33

"Everything I need is added to me."
Matthew 6:33

"Every time I ask, I receive."
Matthew 7:8

"When I knock, it is opened to me."
Matthew 7:8

"People recognize the good fruit I produce."
Matthew 7:20

"My house is built on The Rock."
Matthew 7:25

"I teach with authority"
Matthew 7:29

"Jesus took my infirmities and bare my sicknesses."
Matthew 8:17

✞ "...He gave them power against unclean spirits,
to cast them out,
and to heal al manner of sickness
and all manner of disease."
Matthew 10:1

"I raise the dead."
Matthew 10:8

"I have freely received, now I freely give."
Matthew 10:8

"The Holy Spirit speaks through me."
Matthew 10:19, 20

"I endure."
Matthew 10:22

"My Father tells me things in private,
I declare them in public."
Matthew 10:27

"I boldly confess Jesus Christ before men."
Matthew 10:32

"I am received, and my message is received."
Matthew 10:40

☦ "The blind receive their sight, and the lame walk,
the lepers are cleansed, and the deaf hear,
the dead are raised up,
and the poor have the Gospel preached to them."
Matthew 11:5

"I am at rest in Jesus."
Matthew 11:28-30, Heb. 4:8-11

"I bring forth good things out of my heart."
Matthew 12:35

"I do the will of my Father."
Matthew 12:50

"I produce a hundredfold for the Kingdom."
Matthew 13:8

"My eyes are blessed."
Matthew 13:16

"I am cheerful."
Matthew 14:27, Acts 23:11

"I possess great faith."
Matthew 15:28

"Whatever I bind, is bound."
Matthew 18:18

"My spouse and I walk in agreement."
Matthew 18:19

"My spouse and I are one."
Matthew 19:4-6

"With God all things are possible."
Matthew 19:26

"I am a good steward."
Matthew 25:14-23

"I clothe the naked and feed the hungry."
Matthew 25:35, 36

☦ "And Jesus came and spake unto them, saying,
All power is given unto Me in Heaven and in earth."
Matthew 28:18

"I go, and teach all nations…"
Matthew 28:19

"Jesus is always with me."
Matthew 28:20

"I am baptized in the Holy Ghost."
Mark 1:8

"With authority I command unclean spirits
and they obey me."
Mark 1:27, 6:7

"It is God's will that all be healed."
Mark 1:40-42

"I have power to heal the sick and to cast out devils."
Mark 3:15

"I do the will of God."
Mark 3:35

"My faith hath made me whole."
Mark 5:34

"I have ears to hear."
Mark 7:16

"I command mountains to move
and they move out of my way."
Mark 11:23

"I believe I receive."
Mark 11:24

"I forgive."
Mark 11:25, 26

"I know the Scriptures and the power of God."
Mark 12:24

"I love the Lord my God with all of my
heart, soul, mind, and strength."
Mark 12:30

"I love my neighbor as myself."
Mark 12:31, Ga. 5:14

"Go ye into all the world, and preach the gospel
to every creature."
Mark 16:15

"Signs and wonders follow me everywhere I go."
Mark 16:17-20

"The Lord works with me."
Mark 16:20

"The Lord confirms my message with miracles."
Mark 16:20

"I have been saved from all my enemies,
and I serve God without any kind of fear."
Luke 1:71-74

"I have authority and power over all devils
and diseases."
Luke 9:1, 10:17-20

"I am commissioned and empowered by Jesus to heal
all manner of disease and sickness."
Luke 9:1, 2, 10:9

"Nothing, nothing shall ever by any means hurt me."
Luke 10:19

"I take no thought or concern about my
material needs, God takes very good care of me.
I simply seek His ways
and He abundantly supplies all I ever need."
Luke 12:22-31

"I don't fear!"
Luke 12:32

"As a child of Abraham by faith,
I am free and I cannot be bound or burdened down."
Luke 13:16, Ga. 3:29

"All that my Father has is mine."
Luke 15:31

"I am faithful in all things."
Luke 16:10-12, I Co. 4:2

"I do not serve money, money is my servant
as I serve the Lord."
Luke 16:13

"When I speak to even the most hard, twisted,
deep rooted problem, it always obeys me!"
Luke 17:6

"God exhalts me."
Luke 18:14

"I am not terrified."
Luke 21:9

"My testimony is settled in my heart,
and I speak wisdom that no adversary can resist."
Luke 21:14, 15

"I am a servant to all."
Luke 22:25-27

"All things were made by Jesus."
John 1:3

"I'm a light in the darkness."
John 1:5-8

"I am a son of God."
John 1:12, Ro. 8:14-17

"I am born of God."
John 1:13

"The Word is made flesh in me."
John 1:14

"I have Jesus' fullness, and His grace."
John 1:16

"I believe on His Name."
John 2:23

"God is with me."
John 3:2

"I have a well of water springing up in me,
and I never thirst."
John 4:14

"I am a true worshipper."
John 4:23, 24

"I reap and I receive wages."
John 4:36

"I believe God sent Jesus.
I believe I have eternal life, now!"
John 5:24

"I do not struggle or stress over my needs.
I believe Jesus!"
John 6:27-29

"I have everlasting life."
John 6:47

"I do not judge on appearance only.
I judge inline with God's Word."
John 7:24

"Out of my belly, my inner man flows
a living, rushing, mighty river of the Holy Ghost!"
John 7:38, 39

"I am a disciple of Christ Jesus."
John 8:31

"The Truth has made me free!"
John 8:32

"Jesus set me free, I am totally free!"
John 8:36

"I only follow Jesus. I clearly hear His Voice."
John 10:3-5, 27

"I have abundant life."
John 10:10

"I will never perish."
John 10:28

"Fear not!"
John 12:15

"God honors me, because I follow and serve Jesus."
John 12:26

"I love my Christian brothers and sisters."
John 13:35, 15:12, 17, I Thes. 4:9

"My heart is not troubled."
John 14:1, 27

"I do greater works than Jesus."
John 14:12

"Anything I ask for, God will do it,
if needed He will make it for me."
John 14:13, 14, 15:7, 16, 16:23, 24

"The Spirit of God lives in me."
John 14:16-18

"God and Jesus love me."
John 14:21

"The Holy Ghost teaches me
whatever I need to know."
John 14:26

"I have peace."
John 14:27

"I am not afraid."
John 14:27

"I believe."
John 14:29

"I am fruitful and productive."
John 15:1-6, 16

"My actions glorify the Father."
John 15:8

"I abide in God's love."
John 15:10

"I am a friend of Jesus Christ."
John 15:14

"I am chosen of God."
John 15:16, 19

"I am a witness of Jesus Christ."
John 15:27, Acts 1:8

"I am not offended."
John 16:1

"I know what is coming, and walk in the truth."
John 16:13

"I am cheerful."
John 16:33

"I have the Words of God."
John 17:8, 14

"I belong to God, and He keeps me."
John 17:9-15

"I am not of this world."
John 17:14, 16

"I am set apart by the Truth."
John 17:17

"I am one with the Godhead."
John 17:22, 23, Ro. 12:5

"Jesus is in me."
John 17:26

"I have Holy Ghost power."
Acts 1:8

"I am a powerful witness."
Acts 1:8

"I am full of the Holy Ghost."
Acts 2:4, 38, 39

"I prophesy."
Acts 2:17, 18

"I regularly have divine dreams and visions."
Acts 2:17

"I do many signs and wonders."
Acts 2:43, 14:3

"I lay hands on people
and they receive the Holy Ghost."
Acts 8:15-18

"I now go about doing good and
healing all that are oppressed of the devil."
Acts 10:38

"The Holy Ghost falls on people when I speak."
Acts 10:44-46, 11:15, 15:8

"The hand of the Lord is with me."
Acts 11:21

"I am full of faith and the Holy Ghost."
Acts 11:24

"Supernatural doors of deliverance
are opened to me."
Acts 12:8-11, 16:26

"I see the crippled healed."
Acts 14:8-10

"The door of faith is opened to me."
Acts 14:27

"I turn the world upside down."
Acts 17:6

"God gives to me all things."
Acts 17:25

"No man shall set their hand on me."
Acts 18:10

"Special miracles happen at my hands."
Acts 19:11, 12

"I keep back nothing that is profitable to someone."
Acts 20:20

"None of these things move me."
Acts 20:23

"I am built up in the Word."
Acts 20:32

"I believe all things that are written in the Bible."
Acts 24:14

"I have no offense toward God or men."
Acts 24:16

"I think myself happy."
Acts 26:2

"I have received His grace."
Romans 1:5

"I am established in Christ Jesus."
Romans 1:11

"I am not ashamed of The Gospel of Christ."
Romans 1:16

"I live by faith."
Romans 1:17

"I am glorified and honored."
Romans 2:10

"I am justified by His grace."
Romans 3:24

"I am justified by faith."
Romans 3:28, Ga. 2:16

"I am blessed."
Romans 4:6-9

"I have hope."
Romans 5:4, 5

"Christ died for me."
Romans 5:6, 8, Ga. 2:20

"Jesus gave me the gift of righteousness,
and I now reign in life."
Romans 5:17

"Death no longer dominates me."
Romans 6:9, 8:2

"I do not obey sin or lusts of any kind."
Romans 6:12-18

"Through Jesus, God gave me a gift.
I have Eternal Life."
Romans 6:23

"I am not condemned."
Romans 8:1

"I mind spiritual things and walk in the Spirit."
Romans 8:4-9, 14

"The Holy Spirit energizes me
and makes my physical body alive."
Romans 8:11

"I have not received the spirit of bondage."
Romans 8:15

"I am adopted by God. I call God Daddy."
Romans 8:15, Ga. 4:5

"I am a joint-heir with Christ."
Romans 8:17

"The Holy Spirit intercedes for me in prayer."
Romans 8:26, 27

"Everything, all of it is working for my good."
Romans 8:28

"I am called of God."
Romans 8:28, 30

"If God is for me
who can successfully be against me?"
Romans 8:31

"God freely gives me all things."
Romans 8:32, I Co. 2:12

"I am more than a conqueror
in every situation and circumstance."
Romans 8:37

"I am persuaded about God's love toward me."
Romans 8:38, 39

"I am the seed of Abraham."
Romans 9:6-8, Ga. 3:7, 3:29

"I am a child of the living God."
Romans 9:26

"I am saved (made whole in every area of my life.)"
Romans 10:9-13

"I have beautiful feet."
Romans 10:15

"I have faith."
Romans 10:17

"I am not conformed to this world's way of thinking
or its' economic and social system."
Romans 12:1

"My mind is constantly being renewed and
transformed into God's way of thinking."
Romans 12:2

"I am patient."
Romans 12:12

"I am at peace with all men."
Romans 12:18

"I overcome evil with good."
Romans 12:21

"I have on the armour of light."
Romans 13:12

"I have put on the Lord Jesus Christ."
Romans 13:14

"I make no provision for my flesh."
Romans 13:14

"God keeps me from falling."
Romans 14:4

"I make peace."
Romans 14:19

"I always edify others."
Romans 14:19, 15:2

"I am strong, and I help
my weaker brothers and sisters."
Romans 15:1

"I am not striving to please myself."
Romans 15:1

"The God of peace is with me."
Romans 15:33

"Satan is under my feet."
Romans 16:20

"Jesus gave me the grace of God."
I Corinthians 1:4

"God is faithful."
I Corinthians 1:9

"I am wise."
I Corinthians 1:24, 30, 2:6

"I demonstrate the Holy Spirit and power

when I minister."
I Corinthians 2:4

"The Holy Spirit shows me
what God has prepared for me."
I Corinthians 2:10, 11

"I have received the Spirit of God."
I Corinthians 2:12, Ga. 4:6

"I judge all things."
I Corinthians 2:15

"I have the mind of Christ."
I Corinthians 2:16

"I am rewarded for my labors."
I Corinthians 3:8

"I am the temple of God."
I Corinthians 3:16

"All things are mine."
I Corinthians 3:21, 22

"I belong to Christ."
I Corinthians 3:23

"I am an example for other Christians to follow."
I Corinthians 4:16

"The Kingdom of God is in power."
I Corinthians 4:20

"Christ was sacrificed for me."
I Corinthians 5:7

"I am joined to the Lord."
I Corinthians 6:14

"I am the temple of the Holy Ghost."
I Corinthians 6:19

" I glorify God in my body."
I Corinthians 6:20

"I am Christ's servant."
I Corinthians 7:22

"In love, I edify others."
I Corinthians 8:1

"I live out of the Gospel."
I Corinthians 9:14

"I am free from all men."
I Corinthians 9:19

"I win an incorruptible crown for my race."
I Corinthians 9:24, 25

"I keep my body under subjection."
I Corinthians 9:27

"God has made me a way of escape."
I Corinthians 10:13

"I judge myself."
I Corinthians 11:31

"I care for my brothers and sisters."
I Corinthians 12:25

"I love people."
I Corinthians 13:1-13

"I build myself up praying in tongues."
I Corinthians 14:4

✝ "I thank my God, I speak with tongues
more than ye all:"
I Corinthians 14:18

"God continually gives me the victory
through Jesus Christ."
I Corinthians 15:57, II Co. 2:14

"I stand fast in the faith."
I Corinthians 16:13, II Co. 1:24

"I am not ignorant of Satan's devices."
II Corinthians 2:11

"My sufficiency is of God."
II Corinthians 3:5

"I have liberty in the Spirit of the Lord."
II Corinthians 3:17

"I faint not."
II Corinthians 4:1, II Co. 4:16

"I have this treasure in my body."
II Corinthians 4:7

"I am not forsaken and cannot be destroyed."
II Corinthians 4:9

"The life of Jesus is manifest in my physical body."
II Corinthians 4:11

"I have the spirit of faith."
II Corinthians 4:13

"God has raised me up."
II Corinthians 4:14

"All things are for my sake."
II Corinthians 4:15

"I look at eternal things."
II Corinthians 4:18

"I walk by faith."
II Corinthians 5:7

"I am an ambassador for Christ."
II Corinthians 5:20

"I am the righteousness of God in Christ."
II Corinthians 5:21

"I have all."
II Corinthians 6:10, Phlp. 4:18

☦ "For ye know the grace of our Lord Jesus Christ, that, though He was rich, yet for your sakes He became poor, that ye through His poverty might be rich."
II Corinthians 8:9

"I pull down the devil's strongholds."
II Corinthians 10:4

"I cast down every high thing
that comes against The Word of God."
II Corinthians 5:5

"His grace is sufficient for me."
II Corinthians 12:9

"When I am feeling weak, I know I am strong."
II Corinthians 12:10

"I live by the power of God."
II Corinthians 13:4

"I am delivered from this present world."
Galatians 1:4

"Jesus is revealed in me."
Galatians 1:16

"I am justified by Christ."
Galatians 2:17

"Christ has redeemed me from the curse of the law."
Galatians 3:13

"I have the promises of God."
Galatians 3:22

"I am a child of God."
Galatians 3:26

"I am Abraham's seed, and an heir
according to the promise."
Galatians 3:29

"I am an heir of God."
Galatians 4:7

"I am a child of the promise."
Galatians 4:28

"I stand fast in the liberty in Christ."
Galatians 5:1, 13

"I walk in the Spirit."
Galatians 5:16

"I am led by the Spirit."
Galatians 5:18

"I operate in love, joy, peace, longsuffering,
gentleness, goodness, faith, meekness,
and temperance."
Galatians 5:22, 23

"I have crucified my own flesh."
Galatians 5:24

"I bear others' burdens."
Galatians 6:2

"I am not weary doing good things."
Galatians 6:9

"I do good to all men."
Galatians 6:10

"I already have all spiritual blessings."
Ephesians 1:3

"I know the mystery of God's will."
Ephesians 1:9, 5:17

"I have the spirit of wisdom and revelation."
Ephesians 1:17

"All things are under my feet."
Ephesians 1:22

"I have been made alive, and energized."
Ephesians 2:1, 5

"I am God's workmanship."
Ephesians 2:10

"I am a citizen of the house of God."
Ephesians 2:19

"I have boldness and confidence."
Ephesians 3:12

"I know the love of Christ."
Ephesians 3:19

✞ "Now unto Him that is able to do
exceeding abundantly above all that we ask or think,

according to the power that worketh in us."
Ephesians 3:20

"I no longer think like a child."
Ephesians 4:14

"I speak the truth in love."
Ephesians 4:15

"I have put on the new man."
Ephesians 4:24

"I do not give any place to the devil."
Ephesians 4:27

"I am kind to others."
Ephesians 4:32

"I follow God."
Ephesians 5:1

"I walk in love."
Ephesians 5:2

"I am light in the Lord."
Ephesians 5:8

"I am filled with the Spirit."
Ephesians 5:18

"I love my spouse."
Ephesians 5:25-33

✟ "...Be strong in the Lord,
and in the power of His might."
Ephesians 6:10

"I have on the whole armour of God,
and I am able to stand against the devil."
Ephesians 6:11-13

"I pray always."
Ephesians 6:18

"God has begun a good work in me,
and He will continue it till Jesus comes."
Philippians 1:6

"My love abounds more and more."
Philippians 1:9

"I am not ashamed about anything."
Philippians 1:20

"I am not terrified by my enemies."
Philippians 1:28

"I have the mind of Jesus Christ."
Philippians 2:5

"I forget those things that are behind me."
Philippians 3:13

✞ "I press toward the mark of the prize of the high
calling of God in Christ Jesus."
Philippians 3:14

"I do not continually think on earthly things."
Philippians 3:19

"I don't worry about anything."
Philippians 4:6

✞ "And the peace of God, which passeth
all understanding, shall keep your
hearts and minds through Christ Jesus."
Philippians 4:7

✞ "I can do all things through Christ
which strengtheneth me."
Philippians 4:13

"God supplies all of my needs."
Philippians 4:19

"I am delivered from the power of darkness."
Colossians 1:13

"God makes known to me the riches of His glory."
Colossians 1:27

"I am built up in Christ Jesus."
Colossians 2:7

"I am complete in Christ."
Colossians 2:10

"I am risen with Christ."
Colossians 3:1

"My life is hid in Christ."
Colossians 3:3

"I walk in wisdom toward others."
Colossians 4:5

"My speech is always with grace."
Colossians 4:6

"I am not moved by problems or circumstances."
I Thessalonians 3:3

"I possess my vessel in sanctification and honour."
I Thessalonians 4:4

"I lack nothing."
I Thessalonians 4:12

"I am comforted by the Word of God."
I Thessalonians 4:18

"I have on the breastplate of faith and love."
I Thessalonians 5:8

"I do not promote evil, but always follow after good."
I Thessalonians 5:15

"I pray without ceasing."
I Thessalonians 5:17

"I give thanks in everything."
I Thessalonians 5:18

"God gives tribulation to those that trouble me."
II Thessalonians 1:6

"I have everlasting consolation and a good hope."
II Thessalonians 2:16

✝ "And that we may be delivered from unreasonable
and wicked men: for all men have not faith.
But the Lord is faithful, Who shall stablish you,
and keep you from evil."
II Thessalonians 3:2, 3

"I am not weary."
II Thessalonians 3:13

"The Lord Himself gives me peace."
II Thessalonians 3:16

"Christ Jesus has enabled me."
I Timothy 1:12

"I have obtained mercy."
I Timothy 1:16

"I war a good warfare."
I Timothy 1:18

"I pray for all those in authority."
I Timothy 2:1, 2

"My profiting appears to all."
I Timothy 4:15

"I fight the good fight of faith."
I Timothy 6:12

✟ "For God hath not given us the spirit of fear;
but of power, and of love, and of a sound mind."
II Timothy 1:7

"I have understanding in all things."
II Timothy 2:7

"I rightly divide the Word of God."
II Timothy 2:15

"The Lord delivers me out of every bad situation."
II Timothy 3:11

"I am thoroughly furnished for every good work."
II Timothy 3:17

"I am instant in season and out of season."
II Timothy 4:2

"I do the work of an evangelist."
II Timothy 4:5

"I will fight a good fight, I will finish my course,
I will keep the faith."
II Timothy 4:7

"The Lord will deliver me from every evil work,
and will preserve me."
II Timothy 4:18

"All things are pure to me."
Titus 1:15

"I am justified."
Titus 3:7

"I rest in God."
Hebrews 4:9-11

✞ "Let us hold fast the profession of our faith without
wavering; (for He is faithful that promised;)"
Hebrews 10:23

"I am patient."
Hebrews 10:36

"I can not be shaken, I will remain."
Hebrews 12:27

✞ "...for He hath said, I will never leave thee,
nor forsake thee. So that we may boldly say,
The Lord is my helper, and I shall not fear
what man shall do unto me."
Hebrews 13:5, 6

"I am made perfect in every good work."
Hebrews 13:21

"I am perfect, completed,
and not in need of anything."
James 1:4

"I am submitted to God."
James 4:7

"I resist the devil and he flees from me."
James 4:7

"God lifts me up."
James 4:10

"My prayers avail much."
James 4:16

"By Jesus' stripes I have been healed."
I Peter 2:24

"I am not troubled about anything."
I Peter 3:14

"I am armed with the mind of Christ."
I Peter 4:1

"Casting all your care upon Him;
for He careth for you."
I Peter 5:7

"I have all things that pertain to life and godliness."
II Peter 1:3

"I am delivered from every temptation."
II Peter 2:9

"I am blameless."
II Peter 3:14

"I have fellowship with God and Jesus Christ."
I John 1:3

"I have been cleansed from all unrighteousness."
I John 1:9

"Jesus Christ is my Advocate with God."
I John 2:1

"There is no occasion to stumble in me."
I John 2:10

"I have overcome the wicked one."
I John 2:14

"I know all things."
I John 2:20, 27

"I am a son of God."
I John 3:1, 2

"I love the brethren."
I John 3:16

"I love in deed and in truth."
I John 3:18

✠ "Ye are of God, little children, and have overcome
them: because greater is He that is in you,
than he that is in the world."
I John 4:4

"Perfect love cast out fear."
I John 4:18

"I am victorious over the world."
I John 5:4, 5

"I am granted the petitions that I desire of Him."
I John 5:14, 15

"The devil can't touch me."
I John 5:18

"The Holy Spirit desires for me to prosper
and be in health."
III John 1:2

"My soul prospers and continue to prosper."
III John 1:2

"I am built up in the Holy Ghost."
Jude 1:20

"I keep myself in the love of God."
Jude 1:21

"I am a king and priest of God."
Revelation 1:6, 5:10

"I overcome."
Revelation 2:26, 3:5

"I have power over the nations."
Revelation 2:26

"I am spiritually hot concerning the things of God."
Revelation 3:15, 16

"I reign on the earth."
Revelation 5:10

✟ "And they overcame him by the blood of the Lamb,
and the word of their testimony…"
Revelation 12:11

"I follow the Lamb wherever He goes."
Revelation 14:4

"I am blessed as I do His commands."
Revelation 22:14

≈ • ≈

"Study your Bible daily. Get the power of the truths
and promises found in God's Word settled down in
your spirit. KNOW WHAT GOD SAID, and KNOW
WHAT YOU BELIEVE.

Confess all these promises daily over your own life
and the lives of your loved ones, friends and co-
workers. Confess them over your community, your
city, state and country.

Rise up Man or Woman of God in love, power and
authority then…

GO CHANGE YOUR WORLD FOR JESUS!"

NOTES:_____

_____

_____

_____

_____

_____

_____

_____

_____

_____

_____

_____

_____

_____

_____

_____

_____

_____

_____

_____

_____

PRAYER REQUESTS _____

_____

_____

_____

_____

_____

_____

_____

_____

_____

_____

_____

_____

_____

_____

_____

_____

_____

_____

_____

_____

CONFESSION _____

_____

_____

_____

_____

_____

_____

_____

_____

_____

_____

_____

_____

_____

_____

_____

_____

_____

_____

_____

ANSWERED PRAYERS _____

_____

_____

_____

_____

_____

_____

_____

_____

_____

_____

_____

_____

_____

_____

_____

_____

_____

_____

_____

_____

Famous Quotes
on Confessing God's Word

"Death and life are in the power of the tongue: and they that love it shall eat the fruit thereof."

- Proverbs 18:21

~

"Thou shalt also decree a thing, and it shall be established unto thee: and the light shall shine upon thy ways." - Job 22:28

~

"We having the same spirit of faith, according as it is written, I believed, and therefore have I spoken; we also believe, and therefore speak;" - II Corinthians 4:13

~

"Confession is faith's way of expressing itself. Faith's confession creates reality. It is always possible to tell if a person is believing right by what he says."

Kenneth E. Hagin
Christian Author,
Prophet and Teacher
1917-2003

~

"This is the kind of God we have all the time, a God who knows, a God who acts, and brings things to pass when we believe. Dare to believe, and then dare to speak, and you shall have whatsoever you say if you doubt not."

Smith Wigglesworth
British Evangelist
1859-1947

~

"Just believe what God says that Jesus has done for you, body, soul, and spirit - think about it, talk about it, sing about it, shout about it, and the praise cure has begun."

Dr. Lillian B. Yeomans
Physician, Missionary and Teacher
1861-1942

~

"God's best is for the believer to take His Word that says he is healed, put that Word in his heart, confess it with his lips, and allow it to be medicine to his flesh."

Jerry Savelle
Evangelist and Teacher
1947-present

THE POWER PACK

When I am on the field speaking our ministry promotes what I call, "The Power Pack"

This pack contains the following 5 books.

These books were written by some of the Generals in the Army of God and are full of invaluable information and Spiritual revelation concerning ministry and operating in the kingdom of God.

All of these can be purchased at most Christian Bookstores, or by contacting this ministry.

1. The Wonderful Name of Jesus by E.W. Kenyon

2. The Walk of the Spirit the Walk of Power by Dave Roberson

3. Listen to Me, Satan! by Carlos Annacondia

4. Healing the Sick by T.L. Osborn

5. Triumphant Church by Kenneth E. Hagin

More books by the author:

▶In the Secret Place of THE MOST HIGH

(Spanish version)
▶ En el lugar secreto del ALTISIMO

(Kiswahili version)
▶ Mahali pa siri ya juu zaidi ya yote

▶ The CONFESSIONS of
a VICTORIOUS BELIEVER

▶ My God Shall SUPPLY

▶ Sound from Heaven
Speaking in Tongues for a Victorious Life

▶ Lace, Lust & Lies
Our Shameful Affair with the Porn Inustry

For a complete list of books, more information about this ministry, or if you would like to support us as we take jesus to the nations of the world, write to:

Aaron Jones Global Net Ministries
PO Box 742
Sapulpa, Oklahoma 74067
Email: *AaronPreachToTheWorld@yahoo.com*

Aaron is also an accomplished Wildlife & Christian Artist.

To see more go to
www.WildArtByAaron.com

or find me on Facebook at
www.facebook.com/wildartbyaaron